[3]

→ Definition

Introduction

Addiction is a condition that is triggered inside the brain which may be psychological and/or physiological in nature. Addiction is often helped by the neurotransmitter dopamine, more commonly known as the happy hormone. When you do something new or something that makes you happy, your brain jumpstarts the reward system making you feel joy or fulfillment after a certain stimulus.

The joy is the reward you get for that stimulus.

When that reward system is stimulated, electrical responses in your brain release dopamine through the synapses (or pathways) to the dopamine receptors.

Dopamine receptors close or decrease over time (increase in tolerance) as your brain's defense mechanism from something you do excessively - like eating too much, drinking too much, or smoking too much.

With abundant dopamine but fewer receptors, you take in more of the substance or do an action more frequently in order to get the *same* stimulation or happy feeling you got the first few times you engaged with the stimulus.

This means that your threshold has increased its capacity, and you have become more tolerant to that stimulus. You need to up your dose!

Consequently, your rewards system has gotten more difficult to undergo its cycle.

[6]

Rewards System

Rewards can come in various forms.

As long as they are attractive and motivational for a person, they can be considered rewards.

Rewards can be primary, intrinsic, or extrinsic.

Primary rewards satisfy our basic needs such as for food and water.

Intrinsic rewards are intrinsically pleasurable stimulants that are attractive to an individual.

Meanwhile, extrinsic rewards are motivational stimulants that are not necessarily intrinsically pleasurable - like getting money for a reward - but have become pleasurable due to associative learning.

There are parts of the brain called hedonic hotspots that determine which stimulants are intrinsically pleasurable to humans.

A reward can elicit three kinds of responses:

- Liking or a core reaction to the stimulus
- Wanting or the persistent motivation to engage with the stimulus
- Learning, which also contributes to the motivation and self-improvement (not necessarily positive) of the person.

At times, wanting consumes a person more than liking because the latter dominates the former.

An intense wanting can be the trigger for maladaptive practices and dependence, while liking dominates during the consummation of an action on the stimulus.

Because rewards are diverse, there are a lot of things in the world that can lead to addiction.

Some people are lucky enough to have turned their addictions to something positive, while others have sunk into a vicious cycle of maladaptive practices.

Addiction Is Partly Hereditary

There is now a test that identifies whether someone has the DNA for propensity towards addiction.

There is a hereditary coding of alcoholics and addicts.

This genetic makeup determines how the body processes and breaks down alcohol or drugs in the system.

This Y element differentiates the recovering addict from the drug abuser.

A recovering addict born with the DNA coding, or Y element, is comparable to the person who is born with the predisposition for cancer, diabetes, or lupus.

It does not matter whether the addicting drugs are recommended by a physician or bought unlawfully.

There are exceptions to this hereditary predisposition rule.

While the kids of addicts will likely have the addiction gene, in some circumstances it might skip a generation or 2.

However, some who do not have the genetic coding for dependency, will likewise become addicted.

Why?

Drugs like crack cocaine have been designed in labs to purposefully cross over this genetic line and become habit forming.

This drug causes someone to bottom out at a much faster pace.

The Y element is a gene transcription called FosB (delta FosB), which determines if you are more prone to developing or worsening an addiction, whether drug-related or behavioral (usually linked to the learning response to rewards).

FosB becomes overexpressed when you become a chronic user of the stimulant (whether drug, nicotine, or other stimulants). Inhibitors of fosB are still being studied.

The more typical and palpable signs of developing addiction are craving for more of the stimulant or drug, increased mental tolerance to direct exposure, and withdrawal symptoms in the absence of the stimulus.

Dependency and Craving

"Addicts" refer to people who have developed a dependency on any drug or stimulation.

A dependency is a frantically strong longing for something - an unusual kinky fascination for things.

It is characterized by increased tolerance to the stimulant, display of withdrawal symptoms, and persistent and insatiable wanting.

Most of the time, a dependent user has developed the thinking that he or she cannot function well without the drug.

There are two kinds of dependency. There is the physical addiction and mental dependency or pseudo-addiction.

Physical dependency is an addiction in which the addict becomes physically dependent on intoxicating compounds or drugs.

Physical dependence shows particular withdrawal signs when drug use is unexpectedly terminated.

Opioids, alcohol, benzodiazepines, nicotine, and barbiturates are addicting drugs recognized for their ability to induce physical dependence.

Meanwhile, mental dependency refers to the emotional hold of the drug or stimulant on the addict.

The addict may show psychological signs such as anxiety, dissatisfaction, and demotivation when he or she is forced to cease taking the drug or stimulant. Non-drug stimulants include sex, pornography, and even food.

Medical studies have revealed that every individual to some extent has a dependency.

Craving is the incredible desire an addict or alcoholic feels for the drug.

Fall back triggers can develop powerful emotional and physical responses that can lead up to unbelievable urges to use drugs and alcohol once more.

Craving mostly occurs in the brain where dopamine and dopamine receptors are highly involved.

Another physiological manifestation of craving is in the liver and bloodstream.

Drugs and other orally-induced stimulants (like food) are broken down in the body for the body to use up as fuel, or be eliminated due to their toxicity.

Unfortunately, some drugs cannot be purely broken down and processed in the liver. As such, they leave debris called metabolites. This debris can stay in the body for years, especially if the user has excessive fatty tissues.

Because the drug debris are ever-present in the user's body, it can be triggered anytime.

Heated fights, violent tirades, and physical activities (like exercise) can trigger the movement of the metabolites into the bloodstream and cause the user to crave.

True Addiction and Pseudo-addiction

Pseudo-addiction was initially coined to refer to hospital patients undergoing medication.

Now, it refers to individuals with drug-desire behaviors for items or activities not considered physically addictive.

However, the individual experiences real pain or other symptoms in such cases.

Regular behavior is resumed immediately after the discomfort has diminished.

Meanwhile, true addiction refers to a complex condition in which an individual never seems to be satiated even after the discomfort has diminished. Both addicts undergo the wanting and liking cycle.

However, the divergent point between pseudo-addicts and true addicts is satiation.

For pseudo-addicts, once they get what they want, they stop their violent or maladaptive behaviors. For the true addict however, wanting never ceases.

The following are examples of pseudo-addictions:

- Love Addiction -- a disorder where individuals repeatedly become involved in codependent relationships, enmeshed, intense, even when those relationships or partners are destructive.
- Sexual Anorexia -- a disorder in which individuals become controlled and obsessed with the emotional, physical, and mental task of preventing sex.
- Romance Addiction -- a condition in which individuals become consumed with the intrigue and the pursuit of romance and thrive on the excitement of the chase, but

find it impossible to sustain an intimate relationship with another individual.

- Sex Addiction -- a disorder where individuals end up becoming obsessed with sexually-related, uncontrollable self-defeating maladaptive behaviors.

Does this mean that all people who are newly in love have an addiction? How can we distinguish between addiction and healthy relationships?

Like other kinds of addictive conditions and lifestyle conditions such as chemical dependency, pathological gambling, eating conditions, and religious addiction sexual dependence is identified by an addicting cycle of:

- Shame and guilt that perpetuates a maladaptive belief system of impaired thinking and unmanageability.
- Loss of control and misery.
- Having obsession or fixations.
- Compulsive behaviors.

Generally speaking, true addiction in any form has four major manifestations:

- User has developed an emotional dependence on the stimulant.
- User has developed a physical dependence on the stimulant, such that his body must have it to perform normally.

- User cannot get off the hook without developing a withdrawal syndrome.
- User has developed a tolerance to the stimulant.

Substance and Non-Substance Addiction

Substance addiction is the stigmatized neuropsychiatric disorder that develops due to drug abuse.

Known substances are:

- alcohol
- nicotine or tobacco
- opiates or drugs derived from opium - originally a pain killer (such as heroin, morphine, codeine)
- opiods or opiate-like drugs meant to be pain killers (such as oxycodone, hydrocodone, pethidine, hydromorphone, fentanyl)
- psychedelic drugs or hallucination-inducing drugs (such as LSD, DMT, psilocin, magic mushrooms)
- anabolic steroids - synthetic substances that promote bone growth and testosterone production

Substances can be categorized into how they affect the central nervous system:

- stimulants - drugs that bolster brain activity. Some users mix stimulants with other drinks like alcohol and coffee to pull an all-nighter. Examples are caffeine, methamphetamine, amphetamine, khat, and phentermine.

- depressants - drugs that calm down brain activity. Some depressants are used to treat anxiety and panic attacks. Examples are alcohol, barbiturates, and valium.
- narcotics - drugs, usually opioids, that function as painkillers and reduces painful sensations.
- hallucinogens and dissociative- psychedelic drugs that induce flashbacks and hallucinations.
- cannabis - recreational drugs that usually act like a depressant
- inhalants - drugs that leave a lasting effect to the body because they quickly enter the bloodstream. Examples are permanent markers, glue, and gasoline.

Non-substance Addiction: Gambling

They say the initial step to beating a dependency is to admit that you have a problem.

Handling somebody who has a gambling dependency can be painful. They have a tendency to withdraw from family and loved ones, so what are you expected to do when someone you love has a gambling addiction?

The first thing you have to do is to hide all your belongings, and if this person lives with you, then you need to keep them behind locked doors!

If that is not possible, then take your valuables to a bank and lock them in a safety deposit box. If this person is your child or your spouse, then you need to restrict their access to your cash.

In many situations, people have gambled away their family's savings and children's college funds. So if at all possible, endeavor to get that person's name off the accounts and cancel all their credit cards.

At some point, you will need to face them. When you do confront them, it is important to not scream and snap at them! Just tell them that what they are doing affects you negatively. Make sure that all family and friends are there to help with this.

It is important that everyone takes turns and tell the person how his betting has impacted their relationships -- but in a non-angry, caring way.

This will help the person realize that people do care about him and hopefully will take an honest look at his gambling problem.

Remember, the objective of confronting them is not to stop them from betting.

It is to help them recognize they have a gambling problem and to encourage them to seek professional help.

Some suggest that you try to get your buddy to go to a gamblers anonymous meeting, but I normally don't suggest this.

Gamblers Anonymous is a fantastic organization that genuinely helps those with betting issues stay away from betting -- but well before you are prepared to do this, first have the patient attend sessions with a psychologist or a counselor trained to deal with gambling dependency.

After all is said and done, you must be prepared because the majority of the time the gambler will continue with his bad habits.

Possibly they will make a brief effort to stop just before restarting again in secret.

Non-substance Addiction: Porn

How do you know if you're addicted to porn?

Respond to the enquiry, can you leave it?

If the response is no, if pornography has become a regular part of your life and if you plan your day around it--you have a problem!

A porn recovering addict may tell himself, every man is into porn.

The pornography dependency will impact every place of the porn recovering addict's life but the most devastation is in his relationship with himself and his relationship with others.

[17]

Relationships suffer because pornography recovering addicts spend more time online with the pornography dependency, than with his friends or family.

He experiences residual hypnotic trance where hours spent online looks like a number of minutes.

At the same time, those who love him and want to spend time with him feel unimportant, angry, ignored and overlooked.

Pornography addicts likewise set themselves up for unrealistic expectations in their personal intimate relationships, leading them to be dissatisfied and unhealthy.

The results of this behavior leaves a pornography recovering addict with feelings of self-pity and emptiness.

Without guidance, he will feel depressed and experience lack of interest for life and real women existing on earth -- not just in the world of fantasy, where perfection is the norm!

When pornography recovering addicts decide to change and become 100 % accountable for his life? He learns to construct relationships with healthy commitments, care and mutual trust.

Unlike sex in pornography, the sex in healthy relationships is all about love and connections.

Kinds of Drugs

Drugs are something that impacts your brain and behavior. Typically people start taking drugs out of sheer curiosity. The following are the general types of drugs available in the market:

- Cocaine - a strongly habit forming hydrochloride salt stimulant.
- Ecstasy - a controlled substance used in partying.
- Hallucinogens - drugs that result in hallucination and significantly influences the body by interrupting the interaction of nerve cells and neurotransmitter serotonin.
- Heroine - an addicting drug processed from morphine and appears like white or brown sugar.
- Marijuana - is a greenish-gray mix of the dried, stems, seeds, shredded leaves and flowers of Cannabis Sativa, the hemp plant.
- Methamphetamine - it is a bitter-tasting, odorless, white crystalline powder that liquefies in water or alcohol to form a powerfully addicting stimulant.
- Prescribed drugs - prescription drugs include opioids, stimulants, CNS depressants that are recommended to deal with narcolepsy and obesity.

Substance Addiction: Alcohol

Alcohol is actually a psychoactive substance, meaning it can alter mood or behavior.

Alcohol functions as a downer to the central nervous system, resulting in a reduction of activity, stress and inhibitions.

Alcohol impacts other body systems.

- Gastrointestinal tract irritation can occur with erosion of the esophagus and stomach linings, triggering queasiness, vomiting and maybe bleeding.
- Liver conditions may develop and ultimately become cirrhosis of the liver.
- Other dire effects of alcohol addiction such as how it may cause sexual dysfunctions.

A drinking problem may already be considered Alcohol Addiction when a person demonstrates:

- Drinking more or for longer periods due to increased threshold.
- Extreme wanting that consumes a great amount of time.
- Failure to perform obligations because of the frequency and time spent for alcohol consumption.
- Quitting certain activities to spend more time for alcohol consumption
- Persistent alcohol consumption despite recognition of interpersonal and intrapersonal problems it has caused.
- Continuous alcohol consumption even with drawbacks in health and well-being.
- Withdrawal symptoms such as shaking hands, sweating, increased pulse rate, insomnia, nausea, agitation, anxiety, and sometimes hallucinations because of prolonged alcohol intake.

Here are more alcoholism facts:

- Alcohol use is primarily affected by attitudes developed throughout their youth and teen years.
- Parent's mindsets and behaviors toward drinking, influence from peers and close relationships can impact how one views and deals with the intake of alcohol.
- Alcohol and caffeine are the 2 most widely abused substances in the planet.
- Alcohol is the most severe addiction due to alcohol-related mishaps and events.
- As much as 14 million people are affected by alcoholism in the USA alone.
- These numbers do not include Family members, friends and others additionally affected by the actions of alcoholics.
- Alcoholism can be divided into 2 classifications - abuse and dependence.
- Alcohol dependence is the most extreme alcohol disorder and is defined by tolerance and withdrawal.
- Tolerance is the need for increased quantities of alcohol to become intoxicated.
- Withdrawal symptoms take place when alcohol consumption is reduced or ceased.
- Alcohol abusers are drinkers that may drink heavily at different times and have issues such as drinking and

[21]

driving, violent episodes, or missing out on work or school.

- Alcohol influences appear within 10 minutes of drinking and the maximum is approximately 40-60 minutes.
- Alcohol will remain in the bloodstream up until the liver metabolizes the alcohol.
- If a person takes in alcohol at a rate faster than the liver is able to metabolize, the blood alcohol content increases.
- Each US state determines alcohol intoxication as measured by blood alcohol concentration.
- A breathalyzer field test is typically made use of to determine blood alcohol content for motorists.
- Most states have a legal limitation of between 0.08 and 0.10.
- Different levels lead to progressively harmful effects.
- A blood alcohol level of 0.05 reduces inhibitions, 0.10 lead to slurred speech and a blood alcohol level of 0.50 can result in coma.
- About 20 % of teenagers are considered 'problem drinkers' in the U.S. what this indicates, is that they get drunk, they may have accidents, or they have problems with the law, member of the family, buddies, school or work due to alcohol use and related truths of alcoholism.

A dependency is a chronic and progressing illness and it takes its toll on the mind and body of the sufferer.

But with the recovering addict, the desire to deal with the detrimental condition lies with the person's willingness to admit there is a problem -- and this is where the problem lies.

Most addicts are clear in their mind that the problem is not with them but with the rest of the world!

Getting them to eliminate this thought process is challenging to say the least.

This is only accomplished through intervention or when something dreadful takes place -- that needs drastic changes to be made.

The areas that need drastic therapy and focus, is the mind of the recovering addict, as this is the key system that can determine the success or failure of any attempt to fix his condition.

Substance Addiction: Caffeine

Caffeine is a natural stimulant found in plants.

In food and drinks, it is present in coffee, tea, energy drinks, and sometimes even in chocolate products. As a widely accepted mood-enhancing and psychoactive stimulant, caffeine addiction is not stigmatized.

In fact, it is a norm, and at times quite celebrated because it is not seen as a clinical case requiring doctors or psychiatrists.

Nonetheless, there is such a thing as caffeine intoxication that manifests in nervousness, restlessness, insomnia, agitation, heart rate problems, muscle twitching, and even rambling thoughts and speech.

Liking caffeine has sometimes led people to maladaptive practices like mixing it with alcohol.

The user might think that caffeine will mask the effects of alcohol or vice versa, but this will only, in fact, mask the gravity of intoxication from either drink.

Although people with possible caffeine addiction have rarely withdrawn from the mood-enhancing drink, withdrawal is still possible to happen.

Caffeine withdrawal manifests itself in headaches, fatigue, nausea, irritability, and being scatter-brained.

Caffeine addiction may manifest itself in:

- Fatigue and lethargy without the stimulant.
- Tendency to depression due to lack of sleep, which can alter the brain chemistry.
- Mood swings.
- Difficulty in focusing or concentration.
- Constipation and other digestive issues.

Nicotine

Nicotine is a substance produced from the tobacco plant through a synthetic process.

As a sedative, nicotine can actually make the user sleepy. When it reaches the brain, it can inhibit anxiety and pain through a hormone called beta-endorphin, one of the happy hormones.

When taken in the proper dosage, nicotine is actually more potent than morphine for sedation.

Conversely, as a stimulant, nicotine can trigger the adrenal glands to release adrenaline.

In poor communities, people have the tendency to turn to nicotine instead of food because it can fuel them the way food fuels the body - releasing of glucose and blood sugars, which translates to energy.

Among all types of addiction, nicotine addiction may be one of most commonly recognized type that manifests itself physically.

Addiction to nicotine may lead a user to develop lung cancer, blood clotting, gastrointestinal problems, infertility or problems during and after pregnancy, diabetes, pneumonia, and muscle and joint pains among others.

Cannabis

Cannabis is a female hemp plant that produces marijuana or weeds.

It was originally indigenous to Asia, but planting cannabis has become widespread across the globe.

Historically, cannabis was not illegal and was indeed used as a psychoactive recreational drug, usually to induce religious or spiritual trances.

However, because of its widespread use that has produced addicts-- many countries have made it illegal. As a drug, cannabis is smoked.

Addiction to it usually manifests in:

- giddiness and other silly behaviors
- hallucinatinghearing music or voices
- drowsiness or a great feeling of sleepiness
- excessive desire to eat
- warped perception of space and time

Smoke from marijuana usually pass from the lungs into the bloodstream, then into the brain.

Consequently, smoking marijuana directly influences the brain because of the cannabinoid receptors, usually concentrated in areas related to memory, pleasure, sensory and time perception, and movement.

Cannabis is like a gateway drug to the youth because it is cheap.

Some claim that the withdrawal symptoms are not as grave as withdrawal from other drugs.

Nonetheless, because of the mild perception of the drug, first-timers often tend to try other dangerous drugs after smoking weeds.

[26]

Cocaine

Cocaine is another drug that can be derived from a plant, particularly the leaves of the coca shrub. Because of its powdery-white look, users sometimes refer to it as snow. Historically, cocaine were chewed as stimulants in Bolivia and Peru.

It has also been used by dentists and surgeons to induce anesthesia.

It is known to immediately induce orgasmic pleasure but only for a short period of time.

There are different methods of taking cocaine, so the obvious signs differ.

It can be snorted, ingested, smoked or injected.

Snorting drugs (likewise called freebasing), for example, can cause the loss of the sense of smell, nosebleeds, problems with ingesting, hoarseness and a chronically running nose.

A sure indicator is someone who is continuously sniffing. Snorting is an unsafe way of using, as the cocaine reaches the brain within seconds, resulting in an extreme high but the euphoria rapidly vanishes, making the addict increase his use.

Ingesting cocaine can cause severe bowel gangrene due to reduced blood flow.

This is more difficult to tell, but if a loved one suddenly begins having defecation issues, abdominal pain and queasiness, consider cocaine addiction as a possibility.

[27]

Those who inject cocaine can experience severe allergic reactions and, similar to all drug users who inject themselves, they are in danger of contracting HIV and other blood-borne conditions.

This is much easier to spot than those eating it as there will most likely be needle marks.

Cocaine addiction and abuse may manifest in:

- palpitations
- high blood pressure
- dilated pupils
- sweating
- tremors
- occasional diarrhea
- emaciation
- insomnia
- hallucinations
- cognitive impairment
- anxiety, paranoia, and in extreme cases, schizophrenia
- sudden emotional and violent bursts

If you assume a loved one of having drug addiction problems, it is better to do something about it right away. The repercussions can be major.

So, how do you tell if a loved one remains in the throes of drug addiction?

Cocaine addiction leads to disruptions in the heart rhythm and can cause cardiovascular disease, chest pains and respiratory failure, strokes, seizures, headaches and gastrointestinal issues such as abdominal pains and queasiness.

Drug, tending to reduce cravings, chronic users can end up as malnourished, which affects the problem.

Cocaine dependency can even lead to full-blown paranoid psychosis.

Whatever you do, don't be put on anti-psychotics because you will be changing them from a drug dependency to an anti-psychotic dependency plus the possibility of reversion to the cocaine.

Dealing with cocaine dependency is rather easy if you understand what to do about it.

The first thing is to get them onto a program that does not offer them further drugs, which can assist them through withdrawal in the most reliable and comfortable way, making use of appropriate minerals and vitamins that their already depleted body need!

There is a particular method for handling drug dependency withdrawals that do not make them feel too awful.

Once they are through the withdrawal, a good program would include getting the drug residuals out of their body in the best and most effective way. While they still have the drug residues in the body, they cannot think clearly and have low energy levels, making it impossible to understand the information they will require in the educational part of the program.

Only after they have done away with the drug residues in their body via the detoxification step of the program, will they be ready to continue with the rest of the drug rehab program.

The key thing to seek out in any cocaine dependency recovery program are:

- Comfortable, non-drug withdrawals.
- A complete detoxing program that frees their body of the entire drug and harmful residues.
- An academic component with the person having the ability to develop and improve himself.

Opium

Opium is the juice of poppy seeds, sometimes referred to as toys by addicts.

It can be eaten or smoked with tobacco.

Opium can make addicts feel itchiness and calmness all over the body.

It makes the mouth dry and yearn for something sweet.

Drinking water can usually make an opium user vomit.

One derivative of opium is morphine, which can be bought in pills, liquid form, cubes, powder, capsules, and packets (also called as decks).

It requires the use of syringe, and oftentimes, cleanliness or sterility becomes the main issue.

[30]

As a depressant, morphine is usually used as a painkiller in hospitals.

When taken without prescription, overdosing can manifest in:

- Dizziness
- Shallow breathing
- Low blood pressure
- Circulatory collapse
- Uncontrolled muscles

There are also synthetic morphine substitutes such as Demerol and Methadon, which were initially thought to be non-addicting, but has led to producing similar symptoms as morphine.

Another derivative of opium is heroin, which is widely used in the United States.

It comes in forms similar to morphine and is sometimes mixed with cocaine. It can be injected or snorted.

Unlike opium and morphine, the effects of heroin to the brain are clearer but less lingering, making addicts use heroin more frequently.

Symptoms of heroin addiction are:

- weight loss
- constricted pupils
- often has dry mouth
- often nods off after being hyperactive
- often has flushed skin

- slow and shallow breathing
- forgetfulness
- deteriorating cognition
- occasional hostile and violent behavior

Other Types of Drugs that Can Lead to Addiction

Barbiturates are depressants to the central nervous system and have been used to treat insomnia and anxiety.

Addiction and withdrawal symptoms to barbiturates are similar to those seen in alcohol addiction and its accompanying withdrawal symptoms.

Taking barbiturates in protracted periods can lead to encephalitis, or the inflammation of the brain, or to multiple sclerosis or the impairment of nerve cells in the brain and spinal cord.

The opposite of barbiturates are benzedrine-like drugs, which are stimulants, such as amphetamine.

It is used as a medical and recreational drug.

In medicine, amphetamine is prescribed for patients who are feeling lethargic and patients suffering from narcolepsy.

Ritualization

Normally, sexual addictive patterns are considered as pathological problems when concerns about sexual habits become the focus of life, triggering feelings of shame, sense of guilt, and related signs of depression, stress and anxiety that cause considerable maladaptive social and occupational problems.

We should consider that some people develop dependences on specific life activities such as sex that can be just as life threatening as any drug addiction.

There are many common indicators that people addicted to prescribed drugs exhibit.

Prescribed drug dependency symptoms are pretty universal, happening to a lot of addicts, such as an increased tolerance for the drug and physical dependence on it.

Treatment can start once the symptoms are recognized and the addict understands that he has a problem.

Kicking a prescription drug addiction can be challenging and unpleasant, but it is definitely much better than a lifetime lost on drugs.

One of the primary indicators of a prescription drug dependency is that the user develops an increased tolerance for the drug.

This means that the user needs an increased quantity of the drug to get the very same results that used to result from a smaller dose.

When a person increases their tolerance for a prescribed drug, more and more of the drug is needed to get the desired results. This is a problem for a number of reasons. It can result in death or hospitalization due to an overdose.

Drug Addiction Classification

Despite being seen by most, as some sort of failing of the mind, it is not noted as a mental health condition.

Drug abuse no longer has that classification despite the fact that comparatively less frustrating illnesses like social anxiety disorder and (in some circles) insomnia are noted as possible or acknowledged mental health conditions.

The facts understood about drug dependency reveal that it is a biological and physiological condition, with the body craving the effects that these drugs have on the brain.

The divider between mental illness and drug addiction is a thin, blurred line -- but there is a line.

Nevertheless, current research is beginning to uncover details that are making this line appear even thinner and more blurred than it already is.

It would appear that drug dependency and mental conditions, such as social anxiety disorder and anxiety, are not as unique from one another at first thought.

In layman's terms, when someone divulges indications of being a drug abuser, there's normally some sort of mental health condition riding the coattails, though not everyone who's crazy is a junkie, and not every druggie is crazy.

The mental issues have the tendency to vary from patient to patient, though things like social anxiety disorder are common in teenage addicts -- along with anxiety, performance stress and tension, and a couple of behavioral disorders. Schizophrenia, bipolar and unipolar depression, and other personality disorders are also observed to accompany addictions, though not always with narcotics and other controlled substances.

Nicotine and alcohol addicts also tend to have a host of mental health issues riding in their wake.

Recent studies are showing that damage to particular areas of the brain may be accountable for making people most likely to build dependencies, with the Amygdala taking center stage in the study's findings.

This does not take away anything from the natural habit forming abilities of compounds such as nicotine, alcohol and opioids, but it does serve to explain why some people appear more likely to end up as addicts than others on a mental level.

The studies also found that dependencies for people with damaged Amygdala are not only more prone to addiction; they are likewise less likely to choose from one substance to another in their abuse.

Findings revealed that it didn't appear to matter what the compound was or what the impacts it had on the body and mind were, so long as they had the potential to be habit-forming and the subjects were exposed to it routinely.

Certainly, mental illnesses such as social stress and anxiety conditions and dissociative identity condition can make someone more likely to become an addict.

A variety of drug users can and do claim that external factors forced them into their drug abuse, with several of these reasons being much like things that trigger mental disorder. With psychological conditions now causing substance abuse, is there now need to think that those who are genetically predisposed towards mental illness are likewise more likely to become addicts?

Drug dependency or chemical dependence includes routine taking of psychoactive drugs to the point where the user just can't stop.

The habit forming nature of drugs differ from substance to substance and from person to person.

Drugs like codeine and alcohol require more exposures to hook their users, then drugs like heroin and cocaine, create quick dependency.

Indicators of Drug Dependency

If you are wondering how to differentiate drug dependency from typical depression or mental problems, then listed here are the particular indicators and signals of drug addiction:

- Feeling that drugs should be taken regularly.
- Feeling that you need drugs to soothe your personal issues and depression.

- Suddenly feeling a sense of relaxation and joy, red eyes, problem in concentration, increasing blood pressure and heart rate, paranoid thinking, sleepiness and slurred speech.
- The other symptoms common to all consist of confusion, reduced appetite, sleeping disorders, uneasiness, memory problems, slow breathing and abrupt weight reduction.

How People Get Trapped In Addiction

There are several reasons how any person gets drawn into the addiction trap, and most are not truly ever aware of the procedure up until it becomes too late to take out. Understating a few of these contributing elements might help a person to skip being pulled into that detrimental platform

What Happens

Having a poor self-image is a fundamental issue that becomes the perfect platform for a person to seek out distractions and drug habits.

This addiction is perceived by the person to give him some self-confidence and comfort, which allows him to handle the outside world.

Factors such as rigidity and tensions are much better managed with the presence of these harmful chemicals.

The chemical changes induced by the dependency is destructive to the general well-being of the person, but that person is unable to break the hold the dependency has on him because of the comfort element it offers.

There are also those who start experimenting on these substances only to find that this eventually leads to a harmful and detrimental state.

Wishing to fit in, and be accepted is the launching pad for many.

Drug Addiction Disease

Drug addiction is an illness. There's no doubt about that.

In truth, experts say that drug dependency is more of a brain disease than anything else.

Scientific advances have provided remarkable insights into how the brain works and what drugs do to how the brain functions. Thankfully, this condition is treatable.

Drug usage at first is voluntary. And once dependency develops, that control is markedly changed. Imaging research studies have revealed certain abnormalities in the brains of some, but not all, addicted men and women. While clinical improvements in the understanding of addiction have happened at extraordinary speed over the last few years, unanswered questions remain, that emphasize the need for additional research to much better define the neurobiological processes involved in addiction.

[38]

Current research has increased our knowledge of how drugs influence gene expression and brain circuitry, and how these aspects impact human habits.

They have shed new light on the relationship in between drug abuse and mental illness, and the functions played by heredity, age, and other reasons which makes them more vulnerable to dependency.

New understanding from future research will guide new techniques and alter the way clinicians approach the prevention and treatment of addiction.

When we approach drug addiction as an illness, the treatment choices are significantly enhanced. We can research what areas of the brain are influenced and find the best methods to deal with that ailment.

Seeing drug dependency as a condition can likewise help scientists delve in depth into hereditary propensity to drug use and addiction. That means, we will understand whether drug and alcohol use is connected to our family history and we'll have the ability to tackle the problem very early on.

There are medications available to treat withdrawal symptoms when a person stops doing drugs. But when drug addiction is researched as an illness, scientists will have the ability to develop new medications that might shunt drug use from becoming an addiction.

Just like medications that make alcoholics sick when they drink.

[39]

The Rat Park Experiments and How to Address the War on Drugs

In the 70s and earlier decades, scientists have studied the cause of addiction in rats.

By imprisoning them in small cages with access to drugs, the scientists concluded that addiction was at its core linked to the rat's wanting and liking of the stimulant.

However, this belief was changed when the team of psychologist Dr. Bruce Alexander tackled the issue of addiction in an unexpected way.

In a controlled group, he replicated the experiment on addicted rats in isolated cages trapped with available morphine-induced water.

In the experiment group, he changed the environment of the rats.

Instead of stigmatizing or isolating the addicts, he created a community conducive to rehabilitation without using typical rehab doctors or prison guards instead.

Still, he left the morphine-induced water in the rat park.

He called this the Rat Park experiments, and the experiment revealed that the controlled group quickly started taking in morphine water and in larger doses.

Meanwhile, the experiment group almost never took in the morphine water.

In the study, Dr. Alexander believed that addicts must be treated equally and without stigma in society.

[40]

True enough, many wars on drugs have led to violent and unnecessary deaths and incarceration because of one body trying to control the supply of the stimulant.

Addicts continue to search for the drug under the table and with lower quality.

Similarly, alcohol prohibition in the United States led to opening of illicit speakeasies.

Known simply as Prohibition, the control of alcohol production and sale was received with much violence, bootlegging, and rum running or smuggling.

Because of the lack of support and increased rates of alcohol-related crimes and violence, the Prohibition was eventually repealed.

In the 1980s, former Swiss president and interior minister Ruth Dreifus and her team of health and police officials developed a harm-reduction policy similar to the Rat Park experiments to address the problem with heroin use and abuse in their society.

It was the first time that the Park Experiment was unknowingly put to the test.

Dreifus and her team established a heroin maintenance center where addicts were provided with pure or high-quality heroin and safe and clean facilities and needles.

If in other parts of the country, some addicts were still put in prison (since the policy co-existed with traditional law enforcement), Dreifus' maintenance served like a VIP prison or control room for the addicts.

Instead of stigmatizing the users, they will be treated like hospital patients needing medication with proper supervision. (See Pseudo-addiction.)

True to Dr. Alexander's hypothesis, drug abuse in Switzerland drastically decreased.

In more recent years, Portugal also implemented a harm reduction policy on drug users.

By 2000, the country legalized drug use, and instead took drug dependency as a grave health issue instead of a crime.

Similar to what Switzerland did, Portugal gave the addicts their daily dose of the stimulant, clean needles, and counselling. Some people who were caught with drugs were given mandatory medical treatment, while those who peddled the drugs were imprisoned.

The results showed a drastic decrease in drug abuse in the country. The Netherlands' leniency toward addicting stimuli also seem to work as the country is known for recreational drug tourism. In the Netherlands, especially in its capital Amsterdam, cannabis is readily available in coffee shops. This seemingly hedonistic place greatly attracts tourists from all over the world so they can legally smoke marijuana.

The policy of making cannabis available in coffee shops is to protect users from more dangerous and potent drugs that peddlers sell. There are still illicit drugs in the country, but making the less potent ones more widely available will likely downplay the buzz with harder drugs.

Compared to other European countries, the Netherlands has lower criminal rates due to drug possession and drug-related violence. In the end, it all seems to boil down to reverse psychology.

The more you try to stop someone from doing something, the more they would want it.

In the same way, the more you prevent a junkie from taking his daily dose, the more resistance he will put up.

Some choose to take addiction as a mental disorder that has grave societal consequences.

Although still valid, more and more are starting to adhere to the hypothesis of the Rat Park Experiments.

Our Perception of Addiction

A recovering addict is considered a recovering patient, because he uses drugs too much, or because his life spirals downwards because of drugs.

We have all heard that addiction is an illness, but how do we genuinely feel about this problem?

When you hear the word recovering addict, do you think of a scoundrel, who has unacceptable habits and low morals?

Do you somehow believe that their life situation is their fault and they could just say no?

Maybe, this is one of the reasons why a working Professional, with a drug problem, does not easily consider himself to be addicted and willingly look for addiction treatments.

Success in other places tends to convince the professional that he can also handle this problem as well, particularly when he compares himself to addicts who have bottomed out and haven't been to drug rehabilitation.

Perhaps if we had a brand-new definition for dependency, it would not be so hard to accept that people may be suffering from a condition that will eventually ruin their lives.

In the Mind of a Recovering Addict

The mind of a recovering addict can be rather complicated and harmful as they perceive things differently from the typical mind.

Imagining and focusing on the unreality of everything from relationships to food to the environment and numerous others. It is not unusual for people to view addicts as having divided personalities as they normally seem to be unable to function in the real world with real rules and expectations.

Drug Addiction Treatments

So drug addiction involves compulsively looking for a drug, despite the potentially bad, physical, social and psychological effects.

Breaking a drug dependency is possible but it is certainly a hard task.

You should support your friends and family members to come out of drug dependency either through counseling or through drug addiction therapy options.

Following is the range of drug dependency treatments:

Withdrawal therapy - helps you stop taking drugs by detoxifying the effects.

The method consists of slowly decreasing the dose of the drug or temporarily substituting other compounds such as methadone that has much less side effects.

Counseling - this is more of a psychological treatment that recommend strategies to prevent drugs and prevent relapses, and also giving suggestions to the best ways to handle relapses if it occurs again.

Self-help groups - it helps people control moderate drugs like sedatives and narcotics.

You are presented the drawbacks of drugs and their negative impacts so you begin taking less of it.

Treatment programs - it includes educational and therapy sessions based on sobriety and avoiding relapses.

Almost all these approaches provide instant and long-term recuperation from drug addiction.

Taking Responsibility for Your Life

Taking charge for one's life, the decisions made, actions performed and the consequences are among the key elements that must be seriously thought about by addicts who are striving to make changes for the better.

Duty

Taking responsibility can be a very overwhelming and frightening prospect for the recovering addict, and the support of family and friends would be needed and certainly add benefit if any level of success is to be achieved.

With the help of others, the recovering addict is better able to focus and keep steadfast in the mission towards complete recovery.

Acknowledging the problem -- which is the addiction, is the main step that has to be clearly developed in the mind of the recovering addict.

When this has been firmly acknowledged, then you can do the appropriate next steps towards recovery.

Another key and helpful exercise to look into would be for the recovering addict to acknowledge the broken life and the important things that happened while in the troughs of the addiction.

Also to be analyzed should be the harmful effects this phase has to the life of the drug user at that time.

When the drug user is firm in the decision to look for a full change, the road to recovery needs to be acknowledged as something that is going to be tough and an uphill battle.

Replacing Addiction with New Habits

One of the obstacles most recovering addicts have is to deal with not knowing what to do with all the time they now have on their hands.

Previously, this time would be used in the addiction routine such as trying to score drugs and its consumption? Considering that the effort is made to avoid the habit, the person is lost and not able to decide on what to do, to occupy the time.

This has to be attended to with some sense of urgency, so that the patient does not fall back into the addiction merely out of boredom.

The following are some ideas of what the recovering addict should think about, to fill the space created by the habit:

Changing Your Routines

Taking up a hobby is the first suggestion most people would encourage to the recovering addict.

But this should be motivated only if the appropriate support is offered to keep the recovering addict focused and committed to the hobby.

Making sure that the choice of the hobby is not too difficult and discouraging as such detrimental feelings may push the recovering addict back to the dependency where he found solace and comfort.

[47]

Another option might consist of a change of surrounding and environment.

Eliminating the recovering addict from the comforts and easy access to the addiction will permit the correct adjustment to hold in the recovering addict's life.

Coupling this with activities that take up a big part of their time is likewise essential.

Meditation is also another area to explore when the person is looking for a new habit to focus on.

The meditative mindset can help to calm the body, as it does the mind, and enable the recovering addict to effectively accept new beginnings.

Inspiration to Freedom

Getting out of the addiction state requires the cooperation of both the body and the mind.

This is typically difficult to achieve, if there is no motivational platform to look to.

Having some form of inspirational tools, which inspire liberty will certainly help the recovering addict take the first step to recovery.

Get Motivated

Attempting to understand the problem, which is motivating the person towards the habit, is one way of finding the motivation factor that will eventually free them from the dependency.

[48]

When this has been identified, other possible and much healthier options can be recommended to assist the person towards the independence that they formerly enjoyed before the addiction.

Occasionally making the recovering addict acquainted with the damage that is being caused by the addiction upon themselves, and their loved ones will be a good eye opener and motivational device that can guide them free from the dependency.

This is especially true if the recovering addict can clearly see the damage that is being done due to the addiction.

The willingness to be absolutely free from this miserable life of an addict, is also a great motivating factor that will encourage the sufferer to do his damn best to try and kick the habit once and for all!

Often it would seem much easier to continue at a later date(procrastination) to do the rehab, because support is not entirely available. Hence, do make sure the recovering addict is free from excuses and just do it!

Wrapping Up

Any form of uncontrollable, repetitive habits will often fall into the habit forming stage or category. Where habits are starting to form!

Is would be necessary for the person to recognize this, so that the counseling would be particularly designed to focus on the problem and plan a matching solution that will not irritate the recovering addict.

Counseling likewise helps the recovering addict get the help that is proven enough to ensure results on a greater scale. Seeking counseling to get rid of the dependency is sometimes the only way to finally be rid of the dependency. Or at least it helps them to be on their path.

Therapy helps the recovering addict both mentally and physically to face the problem, and because most counseling session is done by seasoned professionals, the advice and help provided would be customized to fit the specific needs and concerns of the recovering addict in question.

Counseling sessions will generally seek the root of the problem, rather than just treating the dependency with medications and counseling.

This makes the therapy sessions essential and instrumental in the healing of the recovering addict.

Counseling sessions also teach the sufferer to look for other positive and healthy alternative behaviors to prevent reverting back to the dependency.

The authors, publishers, and distributors of this guide have made every effort to ensure the validity, accuracy, and timely nature of the information presented here However, no guarantee is made, neither direct nor implied, that the information in this guide or the techniques described herein are suitable for or applicable to any given individual person or group of persons, nor that any specific result will be achieved The authors, publishers, and distributors of this guide will be held harmless and without fault in all situations and causes arising from the use of this information by any person, with or without professional medical supervision The information contained in this book is for informational and entertainment purposes only It not intended as a professional advice or a recommendation to act

No part of this book may be reproduced or transmitted in any form whatsoever, electronic, or mechanical, including photocopying, recording, or by any informational storage or retrieval system without express permission from the author

[51]

Other books you might be interested in.

Self Help CBT Cognitive Behavior Therapy Training Course & Toolbox: Cognitive Behavioral Therapy Book for Anger Management, Depression, Social Anxiety, OCD, Sleep Disorders, Addictions, Fears & more

The Art of Erasing Emotions: Techniques to discharge any emotional problems in men, women and children using EFT and Sedona

Aging Strong with Grace

Meditation Power Techniques Course: A beginner's guide to meditation for children, teens and adults

The Ultimate Journal Writing Book for Kids & Adults: learn Ideas, tips, techniques & exercises including journaling's therapeutic powers through daily personal self dialogue, prompts/questions etc...

Personal Life Motivation Skills Manifesto: The best self help book to push the motivational switch on how to self motivate, keep yourself motivated, beat lack of drive or no motivation in men & women

How to Improve Emotional Intelligence: the best coaching, assessment & action book on working & developing high eq emotional intelligence quotient mastery of the full emotional intelligence spectrum

The Ultimate Book for Overcoming Dyslexia - Tools for Kids, Teenagers & Adults: A dyslexia empowerment plan & solutions tool kit for tutors and parents to provide dyslexia help for kids & adults

CPSIA information can be obtained
at www.ICGtesting.com
Printed in the USA
LVHW09s1749051018
592549LV00003B/419/P